James...

Where's your spotlight?

Here it is!

Hope you enjoy the experience?

Best wishes
Tim Andrews

Tim Andrews calls himself a professional learner, which is fairly ironic considering he left school when he was 15 with zero qualifications. He discovered his dyslexia at the age of 35. Since then he's been on a crusade of learning to learn, along the way gaining his Batchelor's Degree in Professional Studies in Education. He founded Stretch Learning in 1995 and now travels throughout the world delivering key messages to global clients and at major conferences.

Reviews of *Where's Your Spotlight*

'If only I'd had the benefit of this book years ago! All teachers, tutors, trainers and students alike would benefit from reading it.'

Dee Lester-Walker, Fine Art student and future teacher

'Tim's original and very personal story of the road to learning makes compelling reading...packed with original tips and ideas to make learning and communicating a breeze! A must-read for speakers, trainers, presenters, facilitators and anyone interested in getting a message across and helping others to learn.'

Dr Mark McKergow, speaker and author
of *The Solutions Focus: The SIMPLE Way to Positive Change*

'The complete transformation of how I plan, prepare and deliver my learning events is purely down to the application of Tim's ideas and processes. I have never met anyone with such a focus on the needs of the learner - and the tools to make it happen. The results have been simply spectacular - thanks Tim!'

Colin Gaffney, Facilitator

Where's your spotlight?

How to enhance learning for others

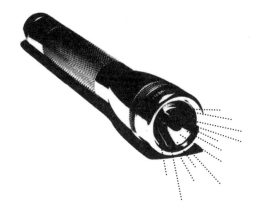

Tim Andrews

First published in 2004 by Stretch Learning
204 Dashwood Avenue
High Wycombe
Buckinghamshire HP12 3DD
United Kingdom
www.stretchlearning.com

First edition 2004

ISBN 0-9548694-0-0

Editor: Charlotte Croft
Contributor: Gavin Burns
Illustrations: Anthony Knipe
Cover photo: Dennis Taufenbach
Design: Lilla Nwenu-Msimang

Contents

Acknowledgement

For Ma and George
who would be so proud of me
I miss them both

My thanks go out to many people who were instrumental in the creation of this book: Anthony Knipe for designing the illustrations and keeping me amused throughout many a boring lecture; Sue Adams who encouraged me when I found anything else to do instead of write! Paul Jackson for encouraging me to put pen to paper; Mark McKergow, Graham Jappy, Dee Lester Walker and Colin Gaffney for reading and commenting on the manuscripts; Lilla Nwenu-Msimang for the design of the cover, layout and text that is easy to read; Charlotte Croft, a brilliant coach, editor and proof reader; Gavin Burns who challenged me and coached me to write.

Thank you for inspiring me...The early days: Walter Blackburn (my coach and inspiration), Steve Tindall, Lesley Hamilton, Ed Percival, John Sanders, everyone at Oxford Brookes University, especially Ros Clow (for introducing me to Accelerated Learning when I needed it most), and Trevor Dawn for inspiring me to inspire others.

In the world of brain friendly learning: Glen Capelli, Rich Allen, Crystal McGill, Eric Jensen, Bobbi De Porter, Dave Meier, Jack Wolf, Greg Evans (Hedgepig), Paul Scheele, Irene Frangs, Leonore Stollwerk-Van De Veen, Gail Heidenheim, Carole Allen, Rob Abernathy, and all the kids at Supercamp UK 1996.

I also wish to acknowledge the support of the clients of Stretch Learning in both the corporate and academic worlds. Thanks to Colin Gaffney, Becky Grangeret, Jean Floodgate and Paul Zonneveld for spreading the Stretch Learning magic throughout the world. Organisations I have supported and in turn have supported me: International Alliance for Learning (IAL), Society for Effective and Affective Learning (SEAL) and European Consortium for the Learning Organisation (ECLO).

Thank you to all of my family, especially Sara who loved and supported me even when I was prepared to throw the book out of the window. Also thank you to my children Stacey and Tomas, who are my best friends.

Preface

How do you engage people to learn more effectively? Chances are you spend hours preparing lesson plans, presentations or sales pitches and the group you are delivering to just don't get it! Even more frustrating is when your learners are saying to themselves 'Right now I would rather be anywhere else than here, being force-fed information.'

This can make all of us as deliverers feel uneasy. This is when we feel the spotlight is on us - in fact, sometimes it's shining so bright that we feel blinded by the light, get nervous and give out signals to our group that say 'I don't want to be here either!' This is a lose/lose situation.

Imagine this scenario – your learners are fully immersed in your learning process, everything has a purpose and they are taking ownership of their own learning and behaviour. They feel safe enough to respond, comment or question and are all fully attentive and engaged in the process. The spotlight is firmly placed on your learners, giving you the opportunity to observe the pure joy of learners learning. This is certainly a win/win situation.

Anami Apaiso, a Buddhist Monk from Thailand, once revealed to me: 'The highest honour is regarded for teachers who can use their ability to stretch people so they can perform up to their optimum limits. People like this are very rare.'

Experiencing this book fully (rather than just reading it) will, I hope, enable you to become one of these 'rare people'. I still have learners contacting me many years later saying 'I still remember the engaging workshop you facilitated. Not only that, I still think and use some of the ideas on a regular basis...thank you!'

This book is dedicated to anyone who has the honour and opportunity to share one of life's great gifts - to enable others to learn from your knowledge, skills and experiences.

Foreword

All I can say is that I have no real advice for speakers except:
1. turn up;
2. don't drink more than three glasses of wine;
3. if things are going badly, talk more slowly; and
4. clench your buttocks!

Best wishes,
Yours ever,

BORIS JOHNSON M.P.

How to experience this book?

I encourage you to wreck this book!

When I was at school, teachers encouraged me not to make meaning of books. 'Please don't write in them, underline, or fold the corners of pages.' I believed that books were sacred and I could only copy down information onto a writing pad. To help you make more meaning of this book you might want to use a highlighter, sticky notes, fold the corners - in fact, make it yours by writing your ideas against mine.

Chunk it...I encourage you to read a chunk, then create a list of ideas or a learning map on the 'AHA!' pages throughout the book. The AHA! could come to you at any time so you may want to stop reading and capture your AHA! in the moment. So go on...read some chunks, re-read them if you like, in any sequence or order that suits you.

Be a beginner...For most of us, being a beginner is normally avoided at all cost. Use your 'beginner's mind' to free up your thinking around some of the ideas and principles in this book.

Learners...Throughout the book I refer to 'learners' - this could be anyone who is receiving information from you - students, delegates, audience, team members, prospects, customers etc. You name it...they're all learners!

Speed is not important...Stop throughout the book in order to have conversations with yourself: 'Do I know this already?' 'Could this work for me?' 'I couldn't possibly use that!' 'I'll try that out!'

Extend the book...by writing extensively, keeping a journal or creating a learning map for ideas you have implemented.

Why not contact me at *tim.andrews@stretchlearning.com* to share your ideas on what worked for you, what didn't work, feedback from your learners and colleagues, or even if you want to comment on the book or just say hello!

Enjoy extending your learning!

Introduction

How the hell did I get here?

I am staring out the window of an aeroplane. The plane is flying me back from Australia, where I have just worked at a huge conference for a manufacturing company. I seem to have had an instant impact on the way they think about their learning and development programmes so I feel that the trip was a success. I am feeling pleased, but as I smile to myself a thought suddenly strikes me:

'How the hell did I get here? I left school with no qualifications. So how did I end up flying around the world to inspire top business people?'

Good question!

I am a late learner. School might be a great learning environment for some people, but it was not right for me. I struggled because lessons seemed to lack relevance. I wanted to be a chef or a hairdresser, and I felt that learning about King Henry VIII was not going to help me to achieve this. The learning process seemed very mechanistic. I felt like I was memorising facts in order to pass tests. My hardworking teachers were trying to fill me with content so that I could reproduce this same content in an exam. They were teaching me the content, however I didn't feel they were teaching me. My learning lacked relevance and *purpose*.

So my experience of school was very frustrating. I approached schoolwork carelessly – I was only conscientious when it came to NOT completing work. I had no sense of *ownership* within my educational experience, only ownership of my disinterest and detachment. When my work was due to be handed over I was often sick, or I had a whole bank of excuses on which to draw!

When I failed my exams, I was moved into class 3B. 3B was for the kids who appeared to be going nowhere, even though they might be fairly creative. I felt safe in 3B because I appeared to be the most able student in the class. This was the first time I felt secure and in control at school. As a result of all this I was promoted out of 3B, not the best move. I then felt as if I was totally out of my depth, right at the bottom of the pile again. In other words, I didn't feel *safe*.

Art was the only subject that I enjoyed. I got really involved in lessons because they were so practical, and also because the teacher was young, trendy and very attractive! I had a great degree of *engagement* with the subject and looked forward to attending each class. The school was a mixed school, boys and girls. I became really envious of the girls because they got to take cookery classes. I would stand in the yard and stare into their class and think, 'My God, I'd love to do that', because I wanted to be a chef. But cookery classes were only available to girls and I had to take woodwork classes. Instead of learning to be a chef, I made a coffee table! At fifteen I left school: a failed chef, with a coffee table. Nothing else.

So how did all this change?

When I decided to go back to school, twenty years later, I started by going to a 'learning support' class. It was full of people with different abilities who wanted help to read and write more effectively. One student, for instance, was seventy years old and was learning to read. It was really inspiring to see someone receive so much joy from reading the local newspaper out loud, and at the top of his voice too! He was very hard of hearing, so he read aloud and we all got to learn a lot about local gossip! There were learners from a diverse range of cultures who were not native English speakers – relatives and co-workers from local restaurants and shops.

One week the teacher went off on holiday and by chance I did some helping out. I started to work with a student from Nepal.

She had been in my class for eight weeks but had not spoken once. I spent fifty minutes with her, in which the two of us worked through the local newspaper together. At the end of the session a tutor came up to me and said 'you've got more engagement out of this lady in fifty minutes than we have in the last eight weeks. What's your secret?' I really didn't know. But within six months I was running the unit!

Now I am able to articulate why I was able to work so successfully with the Nepalese student. I made a real, conscious effort to focus on her and her needs. I made her feel comfortable. I found out what she knew already and found out what she was interested in, rather than take her on an arbitrary journey through Book One or Book Two of the course. I was teaching a person and not content. In other words: I turned the spotlight away from me and what I wanted to teach her, and turned the spotlight onto her, and her needs. I discovered that when you turn the spotlight away from yourself and on to the learner you can deeply engage people in the learning process.

It is this insight which inspires this book. I want to help provoke your thinking around learning and maybe help make learning an easier ride for your learners. At school I became very smart at how *not* to learn, I used every trick in the book to avoid learning. Now I have learned to exploit that same smartness and apply it positively.

These can be challenging times for our teachers. They know how to work effectively and productively with their students, but it is tough for them to exercise this skill when their classrooms are so overcrowded and the curriculum is so prescriptive. Resources are often far too inadequate to enable our teachers to focus upon the individual needs of the student. As a consequence it is all too easy for unlocked potential to walk out the school gate.

Within industry too, I believe that a lot of learning tends to be very clumsy. It often happens by accident. There's media overload in our organisations: faxes, email, internet, voicemail, video conferencing; in such an information rich context it is sometimes difficult to engage learners to the maximum. It is a challenge to make information stick and even more challenging to help learners to retain and recall the information they have received. Yet it is absolutely vital that a business is able to cascade information throughout the organisation in ways that make sense and meaning to everyone. This need becomes more critical and more challenging as a business operation becomes global in scale. Efficiency drives commercial success and I believe we can become leaner both in the way people deliver information and the way people receive it.

What follows is a handful of lucid, practical and powerful examples of how to make your learning interventions more successful. These insights will help your organisation become leaner in the way it manages learning.

Ant

Strike a pose!

Different people learn in different ways. As a result of my experience of applying multiple learning techniques and tactics, I began to notice a trend emerge – the needs of learners follow a pattern. I developed this pattern over years of inquiry: by working at conferences; exploring ideas of accelerated learning; questioning learners; and collaborating with colleagues from other learner-friendly disciplines.

My research has enabled me to create a model that condenses this pattern of needs. The model rests upon four principles, and these four principles underpin and drive my thinking at absolutely every level of the learning process. I really want to grow awareness of these principles because I believe they will be invaluable to anyone planning any kind of group event, should it be a meeting, workshop or training session.

I call the model P.O.S.E. Grab a pen and some sticky notes, and get ready to engage with the following text!

'P' is for PURPOSE

Think of a situation when you have been in a presentation, a training programme, or a meeting with a demanding level of content. Ask yourself this question: After an hour or so, did you find yourself commenting to yourself along these lines?

'So what?'
or

'What's in it for me?'
or

'Very nice, but what do you expect me to do with all of this information?'

It appears that most of us are always searching for relevance. When a speaker says, 'I am here to talk about...' he or she is quite often telling you about *their* purpose, which is usually very different to the *audience's* purpose. Speakers get preoccupied with their own purpose, which is often 'What's in it for the organisation?' But the spotlight would be more effective if it was shining on the learners, who will be thinking 'What's in it for me?' They may, for instance, be looking to learn how to become more confident, or to avoid getting stressed out when directing their team or facilitating a meeting.

If you can anticipate that your learners will want to ask 'so what?' and 'what's in it for me?' and build this recognition into your session then you may well be on the way to establishing a deeper and more valuable learning experience for your learners.

'O' is for OWNERSHIP

At school, I was passive and spent many hours watching teachers deliver stuff. In other words, I didn't take ownership of my education. The only ownership I took was to reject learning altogether. Many speakers are ready to assume exclusive ownership of the learning context – and they reveal this to their audience through standard classroom directives such as handing out complicated resources or setting tight deadlines. We can often identify when a trainer, teacher, lecturer is monopolising control because their learners ask questions of permission, for instance: 'should I do it this way?'; 'is it cheating to do it like this?' This can block learners from an authentic interaction with the content which is being imparted to them. It makes it too easy for any students who don't want to learn; they needn't even make the effort to opt out because maybe they were never invited to opt in. I encourage speakers to reverse the process and facilitate people to take ownership of what they DO want to learn – ownership of their purpose and ideas, written notes, and the potential to make meaning of their own learning.

The language that people use when setting up group processes often encourages people *not* to take ownership: 'don't look at each other's worksheets'; 'I don't want you to race ahead in the handouts because I want you to concentrate on where I am at the moment.' I heard someone say once: 'I'll reveal all at the end because I don't want them to know the answer.' I believe the opposite: if your learners get the answer earlier on then all the better. This helps your learners to build ownership through their own discovery.

There is a common confusion between sharing ownership and cheating! Anything which makes learning more simple, which cuts corners, is great news. I remember at school, learning would be kept secret; people kept the answers to themselves. Pupils would lean over their desk and shield their answers with a crooked elbow. I think that true learning is about looking over that person's arm and discovering as many ideas as you can! If the information sticks with you, it's obviously working for you.

So the second challenge of the P.O.S.E. model is to help your learners take ownership of the learning process and the learning content.

'S' is for SAFETY

Many traditional models of learning delivery may sound something like this: tell your learners something; tell them what you told them; tell them again; check for understanding. Checking for understanding can easily become 'pounce on someone'. Perhaps out of fear the learner may give a correct answer, in which case the lecturer or trainer may be appeased. But I refute this model of learning, and I would contend that little or no authentic learning can take place in such an exchange. Just because a learner has given you the answer to a question doesn't necessarily mean that they have actually learned anything. They have probably only answered the question! So what? The factors most commonly responsible for learning blocks appear to be fear or stress. This applies equally across all learning environments – the meeting room, the training room, the interview room. Its effects can be seen all the time in exam rooms, where

nervousness and pressure impair performance. I imagine many people who fail exams
would do fine if they were able to answer
the questions in a comfortable, familiar
environment, perhaps using different forms
of demonstrating competence such as
answering a question verbally or completing
a diagram.

I'm always asking learners about what makes
a group learning situation feel safe for them.
The most common answer is: 'I don't want
to be picked on' or 'I don't want to be made
to look stupid'. Nobody welcomes being
made to feel a fool or an idiot. Very few people enjoy being tested. Instead, effort should
be directed to make individuals feel more
comfortable within the learning environment. The session leader could add value to
the learning environment by selling the idea
that making mistakes is fantastic, getting it
wrong is brilliant, especially when you get it
wrong on your first attempt. A great friend
and inspiration to me is Glen Capelli from
Australia, a world renowned authority on
learning to learn. Glen always mentions
that true learning is about 'mucking up'.

The deeper learning can often begin when things have not gone to plan, in the process of correction and adjustment.

Inappropriate, unsafe language often causes learners to feel threatened. Saying 'I want you to do this' has a much more negative impact than 'Let's get involved with this'. Using 'we' constructs rather than 'I' constructs reminds the learner that we are all working together, that we are exploring the learning with them rather than they are doing it on their own.

Creating a sense of purpose and ownership is central to a productive learning experience. Cultivate a safe learning atmosphere too and the learning process can be greatly enhanced.

Please note: What is safe for one learner may feel unsafe for another learner, so please vary your safety levels according to your group.

'E' is for ENGAGE

As part of my studies for my degree I observed and coached the students at Supercamp,
an experimental Anglo-American academic
camp for twelve to eighteen year olds. Over
my three week stay I was continually aston-
ished because the learners were learning so
fast – learning about themselves, about others and about specific content. My explana-
tion for their efficiency? Because the kids
were so *engaged* throughout the process.
Engagement is the instruction of the famous
maxim: 'Tell me I hear it, show me I see it,
involve me I understand it.' When I recalled
my first working experience with my
Nepalese student I realised that by striking
up engagement I enabled the learning
process to begin; I encouraged her to get
involved with her newspaper, how much it
cost, what she understood, which pictures
she liked and to make her own meaning of
it.

My own school experience shows the negative results which follow from an absence of
engagement. I thought that learning took

place by paying attention for a long time. I used to concentrate on books which I had to read for tests and exams. Despite giving it my best attention, I was never engaged with the process and consequently the learning did not stick. Compare this sterile reading style with the following intense, interactive reading style a close associate of mine, Colin Gaffney, uses. When he reads a good book he can visualise the narrative within his mind as vividly as a film. Every time he opens the book he is instantly engrossed in the film. Sometimes he is even able to bring the book to life by imagining that he is one of the characters. This is a fabulous way to think about being engaged in a learning process. It contrasts emphatically with a linear and literal learning approach, the approach that says 'I've read the book, so I now must understand everything.'

A productive learning process is predicated on these conditions: the session leader needs to be aware of how to carefully foster a sense of *purpose, ownership, safety* and *engagement*.

When these conditions have been accomplished, then we can truly begin to unlock talent...

My notes

-
-
-
-
-

Ant

Unlocking talent

When studying for my degree, twenty years after leaving school, I repeatedly encountered learning 'blocks'. These were periods when I really struggled to move forward with my studies. I thought that my approach was correct but something was definitely not working for me because I was failing to learn effectively. I went to lectures, listened hard and took notes, but it felt like learning was not happening. I was confident that I had the material in my head, but I couldn't get it to work for me. Another way of expressing this situation would be this: I couldn't *unlock* the learning.

One day, I spoke to my tutor about this problem and she gave me an idea that became the key to unlock my learning. She introduced me to a 'learn to learn' pack based on the principles of Accelerated Learning. It included video and audio cassettes, workbooks and worksheets – just the help I was looking for!

A radical transformation took place in my learning method: I would appear at lectures with large sheets of paper, coloured pens, sticky notes. I would create maps of the lectures, sticking sticky notes everywhere, writing on photocopied chunks of lecture scripts. I would build metaphors and stories based around the lecture content. I would initiate 'question and answer' sessions with friends and colleagues, and use these to explore material that I did not understand. I would fix learning maps on my walls so that I had a visual and physical way to review lecture output on a regular basis. I moved my study to a different room in my house, and used background music to facilitate a sense of private, personal space in my new study. I would start conversations with other students and lecturers in the coffee breaks between lecture sessions and discuss our work. I would take walks in order to reflect on study issues. This was challenging, to say the least, because I came from a place where learning meant sweating and toiling and going for a stroll to think about something was seen as too 'touchy-feely'.

This set of strategies may seem disparate or random. But they are united by the work of Howard Gardner, regarded as one of the finest educational academics in the world, and his thinking was the key that I used to unlock my learning. Gardner recognised that 'intelligence' is really an aggregate of many different 'intelligences'. What Gardner calls 'intelligences' I like to think of as 'talents'. We all have hundreds, maybe thousands of talents. Gardner identified seven core talents (he later added another couple, but I think trying to remember nine things is harder than seven!).

These – very briefly! – are our seven talents:

linguistic – learning stimulated by words

mathematical – learning stimulated by numbers, sequence and logic

visual / spatial – learning stimulated graphically and using space

musical / rhythmical – learning stimulated by rhythm, background music, mnemonics

bodily / physical – learning stimulated by movement

interpersonal –learning stimulated through dialogue with others

intrapersonal – learning stimulated by introspection

The tool of the seven talents is essential for anyone who wants to enhance a learning process.

We all have preferred modes of absorbing information when delivering learning. One of my group members may like to map ideas and information graphically; another may find that reading is a more efficient learning experience. The first step is to recognise this diversity. The second step is to celebrate this diversity – the more talents that we can appeal to, the more likely that our learners will be able to retain and recall their learning in the future.

Challenge yourself to recognise these talents, both in yourself and in other people. By using and addressing these talents, we can really enhance learning. Since becoming involved with these methods I have really unlocked my own talent. Perhaps more than any other factor, it is this process which has enabled the failed chef with a coffee table to become an international educator. This unlocking is a very empowering experience, and hopefully it will inspire you to help the people around you by enabling them to unlock their talents too.

My notes

-

-

-

-

-

Settling

Let's set the scene... You have invited some guests to your house for lunch. It's a crisp, cold day yet bright and sunny. Your guests get out of their car, walk up the path to your front door and you welcome them in:

'Please come in, don't bother to take your coats off. Please go through and sit around the table. Your wine and water is all poured out and your appetiser is ready to eat. Under the plate covers is your hot meal and next to that is an ice cream dessert. Please get started. I'll bring the coffee and mints through to you now!'

As a guest, how would you be feeling right now? Rushed? Not ready? Stunned?

I'm sure you'll agree this isn't a great way to welcome someone to your house! However, this is the very style in which learning sessions are often delivered – hurried, hasty, and with no consideration of whether the learners are ready or not.

I can remember a meeting with a senior manager from a manufacturing company with whom I was to be running a European learning programme. He came to collect me from the reception area of his corporate headquarters and we walked off across the car park together towards his office. As we walked through the corridors, he began to talk to me about the project. This man was over six foot tall and he was striding away at quite a tempo; I was carrying two cumbersome bags, and I was breaking into a run just to keep up with him. On arrival at his office he sat himself down very calmly. As I struggled through the door, dragging my bags, I heard him announce: 'and that's a complete overview of where this project is going.'

I sat there in a pool of sweat, my bags strewn around me, trying to catch my breath. I gasped, 'I haven't listened to a single word you've said!'

He said, 'Let me explain it once more', and he started off again. I interrupted: 'No!!!! I'm not ready.'

I got a glass of water, a pad, some coloured pens, made myself comfortable and said: 'Please can you demonstrate to me using a flipchart, and create a diagram to show where this project sits within the wider areas of the business.'

I managed to slow the learning process down: he carefully started to put together the big picture of the project and within ten minutes I had grasped everything he wanted to pass on.

Settling down

Business life moves quickly and we don't always have the luxury of asking people to stop and start as we please. But this story illustrates the importance of remembering where our spotlight points: his spotlight was on himself and his need to get rid of his ideas and information as quickly as possible. His spotlight should have been on me and only then would he have realised that it was impossible for me to listen.

The situation is similar when we're working within groups of learners. Too often when communicating to others we get caught up in our own task of delivery, which often obscures our consideration of who's on the receiving end. We may need to turn the spotlight on the receivers, to make sure that they are ready to start. There are plenty of techniques to create this readiness. The formal, humiliating ritual of asking group members to stand up and give their names is certainly not going to engender a relaxed atmosphere. Perhaps initiate an informal, walkaround discussion so people can find out themselves who everyone else is and what they hope to gain from the event. Even within a one hour session, it's always useful to spend a good five per cent of the time getting people comfortable with why they are there – get them *settled*.

My notes

-

-

-

-

-

Environment with a 'P'

Consider the following scenario:

I am working with a group and we're involved with some deep, purposeful material. I've used settling techniques, I've considered the P.O.S.E. model to guarantee focus and immersion, and I've thought about the seven talents model, so that my delivery has been diverse and stimulating. Yet something appears to be wrong and I've totally lost the engagement of six of my eight learners. Why has this process been disrupted, despite all my effort for a more effective learning experience?

At last – I discover the reason:

Because there's a wasp flying around in the room!

The learners' eyes follow the flight of the wasp from one end of the room to the other. It is like watching the crowd at a Wimbledon tennis final, their heads going from side to side in an hypnotic manner.

So I direct the learners to take an early coffee break. And I deal with the wasp.

The three 'P's

It's amazing how learners can be so disturbed by such small interruptions within their environment: doors slamming, lights dimming, others talking etc. The optimum planning doesn't stop with P.O.S.E., or the seven talents. We really must make every effort to get the environment right. One way to help is to think of the three 'P's.

The first 'P' is for **place**.
This is the most common understanding of environment. When we ask trainers or managers about their ideal environment for learning effectively they make these sorts of suggestions: comfy chairs; good lighting;

nice décor. These variables are, of course,
all tangible. However, even within ideal
physical surroundings, the learning experience can be impaired. I have seen some fantastic learning rooms, all beanbags, cushions
and cappuccinos. But because of tense inter-
nal office politics, or the use of unsafe language, it's tough to achieve a relaxed and
appropriate learning atmosphere.

So the second 'P' is for **people**.
We can apply the P.O.S.E. model to guarantee that people are receptive and responsive
to the experience. Turn the spotlight away
from yourself and think about the session
from your learners' perspective: does the
process help them to create a sense of
PURPOSE; are they encouraged to take
OWNERSHIP of how they prefer to learn;
do they have the opportunity to feel SAFE
within all learning processes; are they being
exposed to ENGAGING activities?

The third 'P' is for **planning**.
To make sure that a session will be more
successful it is essential to think and plan
ahead. It's always useful to find out who will

be coming along to the event and why they are going to be attending. It's important to find out the secret ingredient which we call W.I.I.F.T.O. – What's In It For The Organisation? I have walked away from many meetings asking clients to re-think the purpose of running a learning event in-house. Alarm bells will always ring for me when I see a client trying to buy a standard workshop to suit their specific needs. They often find it just doesn't fit. I call this 'crow-barring'! The tool a thief would use to force entry into a building!

With some forward thinking I can initiate the settling process before the workshop or course even begins. Sending out material in advance is one way to do this, because this exposes learners to some of the principles with which they'll be working later on, and helps signal a 'no surprises' culture. I call this 'pre-exposure' to learning.

It is imperative that we undertake careful preparation and practice for all the exercises which we are to deliver within the workshop too. Friends from work or home are great people to practice with, especially if you like direct feedback!! Remember the significance of the Seven Talents on your delivery method: experience shows us that we must distribute information into different modalities to achieve maximum impact. However, putting this into practice can be challenging! Implementation requires planning ahead. Research suggests that some learners, for instance, pick up 80–85% of their key learning from visuals and posters mounted on the walls. So these learning aids need to be created beforehand. If we want learners to use resources such as coloured pens or sticky notes, we have to remember to bring them along to the venue. Similarly with music: we should plan beforehand which section of a piece we will play, and at what point in the session to play it.

I remember going on a short holiday with my partner to Greece. We were at Athens airport waiting for our luggage in the baggage hall. Across the other side of the conveyer belt I thought I spotted a familiar face, but I struggled to identify him because he kept disappearing behind the stack of

baggage balanced on his trolley. I still could-
n't put a name to his face so I made my way
around towards him. His trolley was brim-
ming with cases and equipment. I could see
that he had two large poster portfolios, a
stereo system and lots of heavy boxes! I
realised it was Jeffrey, one of our learners
from a recent programme. Jeffrey is a
senior manager within a global company
which is taking their people through some
thorough change experiences. He was on
tour! 'It looks as though you're really living
the principles of Stretch Learning' I said,
with a wry smile on my face. He beamed at
me, 'Tim, how are you? I've been carrying
this stuff half way around the planet since I
last saw you. It's a real pain but the results
for the learners are nothing short of stun-
ning!' He placed the last piece of equipment on his pile and said 'Thank you, I must
go to set up my next session', and raced off
into the distance.

As I watched him disappear, I thought about
the fact that it must have been a lot easier
for him when he used to carry around a
laptop and very little else. However, I'd just

witnessed someone who had really turned his spotlight around from himself and on to his learners – fantastic!

When I first started to plan learning sessions, I would always think about the event itself and what I wanted to say. Now I realise that it's more important to think in terms of what's going on for the learners before the session, during the session and most importantly, after the session. That's right, *after* the session.

Which brings us to the vital concept of 'extending the learning'...

My notes

-
-
-
-
-

Ant

And some more...

People come on our programmes for a range of reasons. For instance, some want to develop their learning delivery, whereas others may want to become more effective learning coaches. This is what the P.O.S.E. model refers to as our *purpose* for attending the learning session. The *purpose* is very rarely about receiving information for its own sake, but about the practical outcomes which can be derived from the learning experience. We call this the *so what? or the what's in it for me (W.I.I.F.M.)?* of the learning intervention. Learners often use these two critical questions to understand the relevance and utility of their programme, course or workshop.

During my school days, I asked myself these two questions whenever I struggled to connect my studies with the real world outside of the classroom. I have asked these questions so many times it has made me convinced that they properly comprise the cornerstone to every authentic learning experience. You may feel that you're delivering groundbreaking content, be it the latest in software development, amazing research results or innovative models of human interaction. But if the learner has no opportunity to connect these with themselves I'm sure the SO WHAT? question will be lurking somewhere in their mind!

We work really hard to ensure that our learning programmes answer the *so what?* and *what's in it for me?* for our learners. But the learning enterprise doesn't stop here: we always deliver the solution to the *so what?* question... **and some more**.

I believe that it's our ability to deliver the **and some more** of learning which is the secret to the success which we achieve with learners. In fact, the **and some more** is not just an adjunct to our consultancy – it's no afterthought, nor an added extra; navigating learners towards their **and some more** is the true objective of all our projects.

What is this magical supplement which exists beyond the core *so what?* of a learning programme? How do we achieve **and some more**?

The **and some more** is the way in which we *extend the learning*. It is how we help extend the learning *outside* of the programme which we're running: how we help extend the learning outside the learner's immediate role within their business; how we help extend the learning outside of their work life altogether; how we help extend the learning into new domains of their world, such as their family, spiritual or creative life. When we go in pursuit of the **and some more** we reach the most holistic level of learning because it is here that learners convert content into useful and relevant ideas which they can apply across all areas of their life. By locating the **and some more**, a learner has a greater chance to make *meaning* out of the workshop or course.

Techniques

There's no shortage of appropriate techniques to help extend learning out of the learning event itself. Common tactics include: recommending reading lists or web sites; forming learning sets which meet on a regular basis for discussions; identifying personnel within the business to engage in dialogue; setting a relevant goal within a time period; determining what the learner will do differently as a consequence of the session; advancing to online coaching or one-to-one coaching.

If any of these techniques are to be used, then they need to be planned, prepared and executed subtly within the workshop. This of course could generate a planning problem: how do we squeeze so much into a session? The most effective way to answer this question is to again consider where our spotlight is shining. When we have lots of content to deliver and only a short space of time in which to deliver it, we presume that we must use all the available time to get our message across. But we need to think less about our needs as trainers and more about the needs of our learners; less about how we can dump our content onto the audience and more about how they can adopt and apply the information which we discuss. So once again, an effective learning experience begins when the spotlight moves from the trainer to the learner.

Now let's look at one of the most useful ways to extend learning for our learners – using our unique talent of suggestion on others. And some more!

My notes

-
-
-
-
-

Let's language

For many years as a child, I thought my mother was having an affair with a man called Bernie!

Five of us lived in our small cottage: two rooms upstairs; two downstairs. In winter, the only way to keep warm was to burn logs on an open fire. We would all sit around the fire, eating, talking, watching television. Whenever I used to go near the fire my mother used to shout out 'BERNIE!'

I could never work out who this man was and where he could have been hiding in such a small house!

After some years I figured out that there was no such man as Bernie. My mother didn't want me to get burnt, so she would call out 'BERNIE' in order for me to stay away from the fire. Playing with fire?... rather a strange pastime, but what else is there to do living in a small village in Buckinghamshire?

One day, she changed her language, and 'BERNIE!' became 'DON'T TOUCH THE FIRE!' Her new expression sparked (excuse the pun!) a new response from me. I began to spend hours dropping paper, coal, sticks into the fire. I wanted to keep the flames rising to my fingertips.

The only reason I wanted to do this is pre-cisely because my mother told me not to do it. The same process recurred when I went to secondary school. I was often told not to do this or not to do that, and again there was a part of me that wanted to do the exact opposite.

This inverse reaction happens all the time with learners. They respond not only to what we say, but also the way that we say it. If a teacher says 'Do not stare out of the window', his or her students will often mirror the spirit of the NOT rather than obey the sense of the words. Learners tend to hear strongly the end of our instructions so they can turn 'Do not stare out of the window' into 'Stare out of the window.' So they will do just that, and take full ownership of their behaviour. Express a directive with a grammatical negation and learners tend to respond with an act of negation. Learners are very smart at turning around the things we say.

Not only smart but sensitive too. They are very acute at sensing the direction in which the facilitator's spotlight shines. I have seen facilitators give wonderfully clear instructions to their group: to stand up; to find a partner; to move to a new part of the room; and then to discuss the session. An unambiguous, sequential, perfectly chunked set of procedures. But the style in which these facilitators frame up their instructions reveals the true focus of their spotlight: 'First what I want you to do for me is to stand up, then I want you to find a partner...'

It is worth us pausing for a moment to consider that phrase:

'What I want you to do for me...'

What do you think that conjures up in the mind of the learner? Again:

'What I want you to do for me...'

What does that tell the learner about who is in control of the situation? Again:

'What I want you to do FOR ME...'

What does that tell the learner about who is the focus of the session – the speaker or the audience?

I once witnessed some control language (sometimes referred to as smart-ass language!) by a company facilitator. He revealed a mneumonic on a flip chart – a model of coaching where the first letter of each word in a sequence create a word down the page. He asked the group about the first section in the sequence –

'What do you think the S stands for?'
The group looked confused, then someone
helped him out by saying 'Selection?'

'No,' he said, with his hand stretched out
towards the individual like a policeman stop-
ping a motorist.

Someone else said, in a quivering voice,
'Start?'

He replied with the same answer – 'No!'

The spotlight was well and truly dazzling
him.

The group were forced into a no win situation, until the master revealed his secret –
'S stands for....' and he wrote it up and
explained what it meant. Then things got
worse. He asked the group, 'What do you
think the M stands for?'

You could hear a pin drop in the room.

Not one individual answered his question.
They simply didn't want to be made a fool of

if their answer was incorrect. So, they just sat and looked at him. 'Are you all asleep?' he retorted. Still nothing. 'Well, actually it stands for...'

This was a great demonstration of the 'I'm in control, look how much I know and see if you can guess' scenario. Sound familiar?

Unskilled presenters use this technique on a regular basis. Imagine if he'd used more engaging language, perhaps:

'Here's a great model for you to discover. Let's take the 'S'. What could the 'S' mean to you in this particular model? Turn to someone and discuss.'

This style of questioning helps the learner to build their own PURPOSE for the model. They are taking ownership for their discovery. It is certainly a lot safer for the learners in a group setting, and working in pairs or groups will help them to ENGAGE in the process. All of this helps the learners to take their learning to a deeper, meaningful level and then reveal what it means to them as well. We call this 'Meeting Them In Their World'.

A facilitator needs to be mindful of the language that they use within a session. There are key constructs which we favour: 'we' phrases, e.g. 'we can do this together', and 'let's' phrases, e.g. 'let's work in pairs'. Employ affirmatives and steer away from negatives: there's a big difference between 'don't forget' and 'please remember', especially when used with people who are anxious about the power of their memory.

We call this **let's language**. It's more commonly known as *collaborative language* and we have found that it has been absolutely crucial to our success. Next time you work with a group, consider how you can express yourself in terms of collaborative language.

Our experience tells us that most adult learners are fairly lazy when faced with learning something different – so to help them, and yourself, think about how you might utilise the power of suggestion...

My notes

-
-
-
-
-

I have a suggestion!

You may want to refrain from reading the rest of this text for a couple of minutes, because we're going to breeze through this chunk on suggestion. However, it's packed with great ideas for you to implement in your future delivery of learning.

Have you been in the same position for a while? Has your body started to get tense? Feeling less energised than you were in the last chunk you were reading? Let's shift our mind and body for at least two minutes:

- Try tensing your shoulders... and let them relax.

- Do that at least three times.

- Alter your breathing. Take deeper breaths and exhale slowly.

- Tense and release any part of your body.

- Now do the breathing again.

For the next part of this process it may be more effective if you close your eyes. If you feel OK with this then, keeping your eyes closed, move your eyeballs up to the ceiling, then back down towards the page, then open your eyes and start reading again.

Feel different? I'm not surprised.

There are over forty suggestions within the first part of this chapter for you to absorb. Here are some of them:

you may want to	**relax**
started to get tense	future
refrain from	**deeper**
feeling less	delivery
couple of minutes	**slowly**
energised	of learning
we're going to	**tense**
than you were	again
breeze through	**release**
you were reading	you feel OK
it's packed with	**any part**
let's shift	they are closed
great ideas	**look up**
at least two minutes	page
for you	**look down**
try	feel different
implement	**start reading**
let them	
in your	

Suggestion

Suggestion is everywhere in our lives, whether it's in family life, advertising, marketing, TV or newspapers – to name a few.

Suggestive language links closely with learners taking OWNERSHIP for their attitude and behaviour in the learning context. I mentioned in the Let's Language section that most adult learners are inherently lazy when it comes to learning. We have observed this in our workshop on various occasions.

Learners form groups and nominate a group leader. They may have a task such as creating lists or visuals on a flipchart. Most groups tend to stand around and let the group leader run the discussion and document on the flipchart while they give them examples to write up. It's fairly natural when learners have a group leader that they appear to say to themselves 'over to you' and pass their ownership over to the leader.

Another example concerns the use of learning logs. We spend many hours creating and developing learning logs that are designed for learners to take OWNERSHIP by making their own meaning of the content and processes that we are delivering.

As part of our 1-2-1 consultancy we worked with one organisation to create a learning log which was directly connected to the content being delivered. We even left some pages incomplete so the learners would have to complete them in full for them to make any sense of them.

The facilitator started the session at 9 am, but by 10.30 am there had been no mention to the group regarding the learning log. So, while the group were having a break I recommended to the facilitator that he may want to introduce the log to them as soon as possible. The group arrived back, he held up a copy of the learning log and said 'This is for you to use throughout the day.' To his amazement, only two out of the fourteen people present used the log to make notes.

I, however, was not surprised.

Let's explain what happened in this situation. I can sum it up in only five words: **There was very little suggestion!**

Firstly, learning logs are a tool to be used, so they need to be introduced and demonstrated as early in the process as possible. Secondly, the facilitator didn't really believe they were that important. Later he shared with me that his spotlight was shining so much on himself, worrying about his content, process and timings, that he had completely forgotten the value of these logs for his learners.

Imagine how much more effective the learning could have been for these learners if he had made some more suggestive comments: 'Here is one of the most important learning resources for you to use today' (holding the log up high!). 'This is an incomplete copy of the information from today's session. It may be really useful for you to make notes, diagrams, or add colour to your log as we go through the day. Let's pay attention to this particular page' (holding it up) 'and fill in your answers to questions 1–4. This log will enable you to make more meaning of your learning and will be a unique reference guide for you to refer to in the future.'

The learners then have to make a choice to take OWNERSHIP for their learning and do something with the information they are given.

When we develop more suggestive language we can use:

'This may be valuable to you.'
'You will probably find this a useful resource.'
'Most people who complete these find they take their learning to a much deeper level.'
'This can really assist you in your role as a...'

To sum up, we have found that suggestive language has been *the* major factor to our success at Stretch Learning so...

You could really develop your skills by experiencing one of our workshops!

My notes

-
-
-
-
-

Ant

The what & the how

Every now and then I bump into someone who I coached a few years earlier and I love to hear them recollect our learning experience. Very often they say something like, 'I've always remembered doing...' They might say something along the lines of: 'I remember creating...' or 'I remember making...' even 'I can remember demonstrating ...' Their recollections are always connected to the memory of an activity, of a process, of doing *something*. What NEVER happens is that someone approaches me to say: 'I remember five years ago that unforgettable bullet point slide you put up with eleven fantastic bullet points. Really Tim, it was one of the best lists that I have ever seen.'

There's plenty of research that tells us that learners remember about 10% of the words that are used in a workshop or course. I sometimes even think that 10% is too generous an estimate. Yet when I started to teach, I would spend about 90% of my preparation time planning on the WHAT of the session. By the WHAT I mean what I was going to say; the key messages; the information models; the content I wanted to get across. With diligence and care I would plan the WHAT prior to my workshops, yet I sensed that inside the workshops, real learning was not happening. We know that most people learn less effectively from the words that we use, but we instinctively use them as the primary vehicle for our content. Which raises the pivotal question: how do we create a really effective learning intervention?

When people approach me and recollect workshop activities, it shows that our learners first remember the activity or the process, and then link this process to the content that is being imparted. So when we think about delivering a programme, it's important to consider HOW people will learn as much as WHAT it is they are learning. The HOW is the process or activity which is used to deliver the content. A great starting point for thinking about the HOW is Howard Gardner's theory of multiple intelligences. If we market the style of our content to stimulate our learners' various talents – musical; physical; mathematical; visual; interpersonal; intra-personal; linguistic – then we can be sure that our HOW is vivid, diverse and certainly memorable. Here's an anecdote from one of my earliest teacher training sessions which is a really good example of my priority of the HOW over the WHAT.

My brief was to give a mini-lecture on strategies to help people with learning differences such as dyslexia. I was given an overhead projector and a screen. On the overhead projector I put a nutcracker, a pair of scissors and a bottle opener. I projected these images on to the screen throughout the session and for the length of the session I did not refer to them once. When I closed my lecture I invited questions from the group, and naturally someone asked me,

'I'm really intrigued, why do you have a nutcracker, a pair of scissors and a bottle opener projected on the screen?' I asked if it bothered her and she said, 'I found it really distracting, it kept taking my mind away from the discussion.'

Fantastic! I had provoked perplexity in the minds of my learners! I wanted them to grasp how it feels to be dyslexic; I wanted them to understand that dyslexia is a condition which can render symbols and characters both confusing and antagonistic. My audience were all fellow trainee teachers, people who were both talented and clever, and for some of them this was the first time that they had experienced what it was like to be antagonised in a learning forum. To this very day, some of the people still recall that experience and link it with my lecture on teaching strategies.

This story illustrates that the HOW acts as a vehicle for the WHAT. Paradoxically, it also shows the importance of making the learning experience 'brain friendly'. Eric Jensen writes in his book *Brain-Based Learning* that we learn best when we use approaches that are more brain compatible. I was asked recently:

'What do you mean by 'brain compatible'?
Isn't all learning brain compatible?
Isn't all learning for the brain?'

It's a great question, and to answer it we need to remind ourselves of the prevalence and power of the opposite concept: brain antagonistic learning techniques. Here's a common example of such a technique: use a flip chart to write down some ideas, and as the learners are trying to note down this material flip over a new sheet and make the content vanish before they have copied it all. That is deeply antagonistic towards a learner. It reminds me of the catch phrase of the late comedian Tommy Cooper: 'There it is, there it's gone, just like that.' That's a great summary of a brain antagonistic delivery stance.

If we're really determined to antagonise our learners we should use overhead acetates in an ineffective way. Fill an acetate with too much information and replace the slide when the audience is half way through reading it. There it is, there it's gone, just like that. The most contemporary approach to antagonising learners is to use the presentation software on a laptop computer. This is perfect from a facilitator's perspective because presentations can be written on a plane or train, or adapted five minutes before the learning session is due to start. And it offers the ultimate in brain antagonism: you can fill a chart with a list of twenty-five bullet points, let people get half way through the chart and then make the chart disappear. And repeat this process for fifty or one hundred charts. There it is, there it's gone, just like that.

Let's not antagonise learners by throwing too many obstacles at them. If learners can experience the HOW it will cement their grasp on the WHAT. Think about where your spotlight points: ask yourself if it's really upon the learning preferences of your audience and not on your obligation to let loose as much content as you can. Dr Rich Allen is a leading facilitator of learning to learn, a great friend who I always love working with. He uses a phrase which perfectly articulates how we should think about the WHAT and the HOW:

Teach people first and content second.

My notes

-

-

-

-

-

Ant

It's a frame up!

I have a great colleague called Jack Wolf, and he once mentioned to me that my posters and handouts would be much more valuable to our learners if we printed a frame around them. He derived this idea from optical research, which suggests that the eye tends to linger longer on information that has a border around it. We took Jack's advice, and now all our communications, like our website and our letterheads, feature a strong graphical frame. But how do we extend framing from the visual to the verbal? Or: How do we frame up a piece of information so that people take more notice, and linger longer on the content that we are about to deliver or the process that we are about to initiate?

A learning partner of mine, Crystal McGill, is a master of framing up good practices for learners, and I can remember her demonstrating this at a conference in Houston, Texas. Crystal's session was about group dynamics – where she demonstrates how to move groups around the room. I found out which room she had been assigned and went along early to help her set up. As I walked in she was standing in the middle of the room, smiling. The room that she had been allocated for the session was like a gladiator's pit! There was ramped seating, tiered upwards and her podium was right at the bottom of the pit. To encourage people to move about and meet each other, it really helps to use a room with a flat surface. 'Oh my word', I thought to myself, 'this is not a good environment for what she needs.' So I asked: 'Crystal, how are you going to deal with this?' to which she replied 'I will just frame it differently.'

I took a seat, five rows up. There were more people behind me, and it felt as if I was sitting at the cinema. I could see Crystal in the distance – energetic, high impact, playing music, welcoming her learners. This is how she started the workshop:

'Good morning everybody. We have a wonderful opportunity today to experiment with different ways to move groups around the room, even with fixed seating. Let's move on!'

What a great frame! She didn't apologise for the environment, nor did she share any of her worries with the learners. She immediately primed us into an experimental mode in which we were ready to overcome the problem of the fixed seating. Her one and a half hour session was fantastic and in her feedback it was described as one of the best sessions at the entire conference. Isn't that amazing when she had the most ineffective and inappropriate of rooms? Which just goes to show the impact and value of a great frame.

In a situation like Crystal's we have to make a choice. We can either say: 'This is going to be really good, let's get on with it.' Or we can be apologetic and negative, which risks a downward spiral that could take the group down with us too. I have noticed, especially in the UK, that a lot of people tend to apologise when they begin to present. It could be because they are nervous, or it could be because they have the spotlight too firmly on themselves. I hear it so often: 'I'm sorry, I know you may find this boring but we really have to cover this...' I have a great example of this apologetic attitude from working with a colleague at a large manufacturing base. Her company was rolling out change programmes across the business. Her specialist area was finance. I sat down with her and asked her how she would start. She said: 'I'm sorry, because I know that finance is boring, and it's going to be fairly hard for people to understand this stuff.' I asked her why and she said: 'Because it's a dry topic, but they need to know it.' She had killed my enthusiasm for her presentation, and I had only heard the opening lines! After I coached her to frame it up more positively it was wonderful to watch her present to a group. Her introductory frame was completely transformed:

'This is important for you in order to get the most out of your role. This connects to the wider topic of being aware of the bottom line of the business, which means it will help you grow awareness of how to be more effective and more competitive. You can put these ideas into practice at your next team briefing. You will get the opportunity to talk to each other and write things down as we go. So let's take a minute to talk to the person next to us and discuss 'what does finance mean to you?' LET'S GO!'

It was much more positive and dynamic, and it was created using a model that we have built called F.R.A.M.E.

F is for 'Focus...

On What's In It For Me.' Start to think in terms of the audience, and why they should be interested in this topic. Direct the spotlight firmly on your learner.

R is for 'Relevant'

Why and how is this relevant to the group? Notice that she starts with the 'What's In It For Me?'

('This is important for you, in order to get the most out of your role...') and then moves onto 'Relevance' ('...connects to the wider topic of being aware of the bottom line of the business...').

A is for 'Apply It'

In her introductory frame, she points out exactly how her learners can use what they will learn, hence: '...You can put these ideas into practice at your next team briefing...'

M is for 'Meaning'

As I have mentioned before, it appears that the brain is always searching for meaning and an audience needs to learn how we will be building meaning into the session. Thus she says '...you will get the opportunity to talk to each other and write things down as we go...'

And the E is for 'An Emotive Recap'

It's a great way to wrap up the frame. Try 'Let's get moving!!' or 'We're going to have a really good session!!'

The F.R.A.M.E. model is a really useful way of framing up information. And it needn't only be used at the beginning of a session. Frames work well following the session we're doing summaries, to remind people what they have learned and what they can do with it in the future.

I can remember the days when I was first practising to frame up information. I was collaborating with a colleague called John, who was running a very successful hairdressing business. We were co-facilitating a workshop with some salon managers. Our morning session was amazing – the learners took us on a wonderful journey, and we all really enjoyed it. However, the learning that we covered in the morning didn't quite tie in with the content that John and I originally planned to deliver. So at lunchtime, we realised that we were about ninety minutes behind our schedule. Over lunch, John said to me: 'When we start out this afternoon, I'm going to tell the group: 'Look – we need to speed things up because we're running an hour and a half behind, so we're going to move pretty quickly because we need to be finished by 4.30 pm." I looked at John: he grinned, I grinned. 'That's not a good frame, is it?' he said. It's a great example of the spotlight shining straight upon the facilitator. So we had a quick discussion about a different way to frame up the session, and at two o'clock John walked out before the group. With a big grin he said: 'Right everybody we have got a great opportunity this afternoon to look at how we can become better stylists and make more money. So we're going to BREEZE through some of this information and we're going to be away out of the door by half past four. Let's get moving!'

Our students remained relaxed throughout the session as if they were breezing along, even though John and I were really driving the session very quickly. Because we framed the afternoon up as 'a breeze', our learners felt as if it was a breeze. We can use frames to give our content a purpose, to help make more meaning for our learners, to help them apply what we deliver. And in doing this, the whole group suddenly appears to take on a more positive mode towards whatever it is they are receiving. It's amazing what a good frame can do!! Rich Allen is a great colleague of mine, and his book *Impact Teaching* has been a huge inspiration for me. He says:

Frames create meaning. Frames answer the question 'why?'

My notes

-

-

-

-

-

Switch that light off...

Eric Jensen is a great innovator in brain-compatible learning techniques. Once I heard him say words to the effect of: 'A good teacher or trainer is just someone who is good at managing learners' states.'

I remember finding this statement quite challenging to accept because 'managing people's states' gave me an impression of manipulation and mind games, but now I believe that my initial wariness was mis-placed. It is perfectly natural for us to manage our own state changes: if we feel hungry, we eat; if we are cold, we wear more clothes; if we are tired, we take a rest.

For many years I was a hair designer, and one way of describing the function of a hair designer is as someone who changes their client's state, and in doing so can give a lot of pleasure. So guiding state change is not necessarily an act of stealth or coercion, it's another useful delivery tool to help drive great results.

The Experiment

I once facilitated a big programme and we thought we'd experiment with the concept of state change. Our experiment involved using not one training room, but two. When our learners arrived we accompanied them straight past the room which we had pre-pared for our workshop and instead took them along the corridor to a second, gloomy classroom. It was dimly lit and only had a few small windows. The walls were a dismal grey. It was full of desks that were laid out in straight rows, in the fashion of a school classroom. It was a very bleak looking place. The learners had been expecting a friendly, brain-compatible session, and many looked shocked as they entered the room.

My colleague opened the session by reading out a long and cheerless list which was written on a flip chart. She then introduced me. I was sitting next to an overhead projector and my opening words were: 'I'm sorry, but I have to do this. Please pay attention to the following fire evacuation procedures...' I switched on the overhead projector and threw a wildly out of focus image onto the screen. 'I'm sorry,' I said 'but I've never used one of these before.' After I had finished my apologies, my colleague resumed reading from another long and cheerless list.

Our aim was to make this first classroom feel uninspiring and lifeless. And, courtesy of a wonderful coincidence, a faulty light bulb provided our performance with its *pièce de résistance*. The room was lit by a series of fluorescent strip lights, and while I was speaking about evacuation procedures one of these began to flicker on and off. The flicker became more rapid and more noisy during my colleague's address. This crescendo grew and grew until my colleague was suddenly interrupted – a learner stood up and shouted: 'I can't stand this broken light any more. I have *got* to switch that light off!' And she marched to the light switch, slammed it off, and sat down very angrily. Silence in the room. Lots of unhappy faces.

When the level of despondency became excruciating, I paused the session. Standing up, I said that I didn't like the room and invited the group to follow me, which they hastily did. I lead everyone out to our second, proper room. There were vibrant, colourful posters all over the walls, music playing, comfortable chairs and lots of natural light. The faces of our learners expressed total delight.

We immediately debriefed the difference between the two learning environments. The first room provoked thoughts such as: 'get me out of here'; 'I want to go home'; 'I want to die'; 'this takes me right back to school.' The second room inspired thoughts such as: 'wow'; 'great'; 'let's get started'; 'this is going to be fantastic.'

It became apparent that we had certainly elicited two completely different states within our group of learners in a very short space of time.

We use state changes to chunk up long pieces of delivery especially if the content is highly technical and content rich. This helps our learners to remain more alert and focussed for longer periods of time, yet in smaller, bite-size sections. A state change could simply be suggested by the facilitator:

- Ask a question
- Discuss with a partner
- Take a water break
- Stand up... find a partner
- Get into pairs, trios, small groups
- Please come and get a handout etc.

Learning resources, if carefully used, can also help the group to change state. We use:

- Learning logs (incomplete)
- Posters around the room
- Music for purpose
- A different room layout

When eliciting state changes please remember that learners prefer it if they:

- Have a PURPOSE
- They can take OWNERSHIP
- There is a feeling of trust and SAFETY

Then... you have more chance of them being ENGAGED in the process.

So now can you see the value in managing the state of your learners?

Ant

Less is more

I've told you the story of the coffee table that I made at school. Now here's my story about the seven chairs.

It begins in London, on the first day of a huge, exciting learning event. I am seated in a conference room amid an audience of two thousand eager people. We are waiting for the entrance of the people who will guide and inspire us over this three day programme. On stage: seven empty chairs.

The opening speaker appears on stage, speaks for fifteen minutes and then takes their seat on the nearest chair to the podium. The room is dark, warm and it's just after lunch and I could see the tired and weary faces of others around me. We were in for a long session.

The second speaker appears on stage, speaks for twenty minutes then takes the next available chair.

I am aware that the room is growing warmer and darker... or am I loosing the will to live at this point?

As the third speaker appears I am beginning to find my seat very uncomfortable so I started to do chair aerobics. The type of erratic fidgeting I do on a long haul flight when I'm trying to sleep sitting up!

As the fourth speaker appears I can hear the sounds of the audience growing restless. It was at this point I realised the huge value a state change could have been for me and the other 1,999 people suffering in the room.

Two hours after the session opened the seventh speaker walks on stage. The audience can sense release and relief. Excitement builds with the thought of freedom at last. My thoughts are fixed upon tea, coffee, stretching my limbs, seeing some daylight, breathing fresh air. The seventh speaker begins to conclude his address, but somewhere behind him there is movement:

Enter stage right: a man carrying...
ANOTHER CHAIR.

Two thousand people emit a collective groan of disappointment.

What does this experience show? It shows that although we can deliver more and more information, it doesn't mean our audience can absorb more. If we have lots of information to deliver, we must chunk it into bite size portions in order for our learners to grasp it. Drizzle a few state changes into the pot and you have a great recipe for learning effectively.

When trainers show me the planning sheet for their learning programmes my first question often is: 'How many weeks does the course run for?' They say 'Three days'. Many deliverers start off with too much material and too little time in which to deliver it. What creates this contradiction? It could be that terrible curse: 'but I have to cover it'.

When I hear those words I have to ask: 'But what does 'cover' look like to you?' And the response is often: 'It means that I have to talk about it.' So that's why we often hear facilitators express themselves in terms of what they are compelled to talk about: 'For the first fifteen minutes, I'm going to talk about... and then for the next hour I will be talking about... and then after the break I will be talking about...' The first thing a learner will understand from this is: there's going to be a whole lot of talking going on. If you translate that into the learner's perspective it means: there's going to be a whole lot of passive listening going on too. And guess what? Many people find that a very unappealing proposition.

Sometimes we are accused of keeping our content simple and keeping our messages simple. Simplification is often a deceptive process, and often when we work with large organisations they find that simplifying information can be a very complex operation.

We use the three 'S' formula to guide us through the process.

The first 'S' is for '**simplify**': which information is essential and which is marginal? How can we reduce all content so it relates to our core messages?

The second 'S' is for '**simplify**': we take those messages and simplify again. This is a great strategy for preparing for questions. When facilitators are asked questions they very often repeat their content rather than answer the question. But if content is simplified right down it becomes easier to explain or communicate it in different ways.

The third 'S' is for: let's take the information once again and **simplify**. Remember: more does not equal more. Maybe when you first picked up this volume you thought to yourself 'Hmmm, seems rather short, not much to this book.' But hopefully you will agree now that quite often, less is more.

My notes

-

-

-

-

-

Modelling

So if we successfully implement the F.R.A.M.E. model, we should be able to address not only the WHY question for our learners but also other questions such as the WHAT, the HOW, the WHEN and the WHO of learning. Let's remember both Let's Language and Suggestion, and then we are really starting to model good practice. Let's look at modelling!!

My friends Dave and Patsy moved to Perth in Australia. Dave had entered into retirement and Patsy wanted to be near her family. I hadn't seen them for a year so when they came back to the UK to visit we all met up and had a barbecue. When I started to speak to Dave I realised that he had acquired something of an Australian accent. He had a bit of a twang! This fascinated me; he had only been away for a year but he had really started to model the accent. Then I recollected that even after a two week stay in America I begin to use American words and expressions.

When we are in a new environment, it is amazing how we often mirror new ways of talking and behaving. This idea of modelling is huge for us when we work with groups and it is important from both the learner's perspective and the facilitator's perspective.

I can remember attending a workshop at a conference in Italy. A professor was running the session and I was really excited because he had written two or three publications and his workshop topics looked great. Me and fifteen or twenty other learners filed into the room. In the middle, alone, sat the professor. Amid complete silence. He looked up, offered some vague eye contact, and announced in a dull voice: 'What would you like to discuss today? What would you like to get from this session?' It was obvious to us that the session had no start, no middle and no end. This made me feel rather cheated

because it was costing me a great deal of
money to attend the conference; I had to
take time off from work, I had paid for
flights, hotel and conference fee. So when
the professor asked 'What would you like to
get from this session?' my first thought was,
'I want to get value for money.' The professor continued: 'We'll write all our ideas on
sticky notes.' So I stood up, and walked
across to the sticky notes. Suddenly the
professor turned around, raised his hand
and said in an incredible booming voice
'NO. NOT NOW. I HAVEN'T STARTED
YET.' The audience all stared at me. I was
red-faced and I felt very foolish.

As you may remember, I spent many years at
school making life difficult not just for
myself, but for the teachers and the people
around me. So when the professor made me
feel uncomfortable and stupid I thought,
'Aha! I can model his behaviour.'

I sat down with my tail between legs, and
wrote down 'VALUE FOR MONEY' on my
sticky note. The professor directed us into
small groups to discuss his questions and I

said to all the people in my group: 'This guy doesn't appear to have a structure for this session. I have spent a lot of money getting over here and I feel that I need to get some value for money.' Within a few minutes, three out of the four learners around me were in agreement, and there was a cluster of sticky notes stuck on the wall with 'VALUE FOR MONEY' printed across them. 'VALUE FOR MONEY' had nothing to do with the theme of the session at all, but it was our retaliation modelled upon the professor's own negative language and behaviour.

He found it really difficult to cope with this and upon reflection, it was not a good experience for anyone. But it told us all that if the facilitator models negative language and negative behaviour, then his or her learners will tend to model it back. If we can frame up the introduction to a session with 'This is going to be a great start' or 'We're going to breeze through', learners tend to model breezing or having a good time.

Here are a few approaches based around modelling which work for us: using positive language to frame up the learning piece – this tends to get people feeling positive about learning; sitting down in order to facilitate review sessions – this helps to make the groups feel that you are involved, rather than removed from the learning process; modelling the use of learning logs – we use learning logs along with our learners because this shows that we are learning too.

So if we return to our professor friend in Italy, perhaps he would have formed a better relationship with his group if he had modelled a positive presence by smiling and using some positive language. Instead, he started his session by assassinating me in front of the group and so I modelled him and spent the rest of the session trying to assassinate him. He modelled resistance; I resisted back.

Modelling can also affect the timing of your sessions. I can remember working with a colleague who was learning to become an associate of Stretch Learning. I asked her to demonstrate to our group a poster of her good news. A good news poster is a way of using pictures to show the good things that are happening to you. The learner draws a quick little picture to represent one item of news. This picture can be drawn within an 'inside work' segment or 'outside work' segment. We usually put two pictures in each segment and then we use the poster to deliver our news to the group. But to my surprise, when my colleague started delivering her poster I noticed almost eight images in each segment. So she had sixteen items to share with the rest of the group! We then asked the group to create a poster around their good news, and guess what? – each person came up with eight pieces of news related to their work and eight pieces of news related to non-work. There were twelve people in the group: usually there would be about forty-eight pieces of information to deliver, but this time there was 12 x 16 pieces of information, which is... well, I'll let you work that out for yourself. Instead of taking twenty minutes, the exercise took one hour and ten minutes! However, it was a great learning for my colleague because she suddenly realised that learners certainly model what we say and do.

My notes

-

-

-

-

-

Pont

Celebration time! Come on!

The style in which a learning room is set up is absolutely crucial. I have tried to draw attention to how this can impact upon successful *settling* and upon successful *state management*. So naturally, before a programme begins, I like to spend some time making sure that the learning environment looks and feels more engaging for the learners. I can remember working one evening, preparing a room for a group of people who were arriving the following day. It was nine o'clock so I had upbeat music playing to change my state and keep me from feeling so tired. I spent some time putting up posters, spreading out comfy cushions, displaying books, raising blinds to make sure that the room would be filled with sunlight in the morning. I even draped some streamers from the ceiling to add some texture.

By the time I was finished, the room looked really wonderful. I was feeling very pleased with the overall effect when I heard a knock at the door and in walked a trainer from a neighbouring room. He stopped and gazed around. Then the guy from next door and I had the following dialogue (I'll refer to him as GUY for short):

TIM: Hi there!

GUY: Wow, this is really great!

TIM: Thank you very much.

GUY: So, it must be your last day tomorrow then?

TIM: Last day of what?

GUY: The last day of your training programme?

TIM: No, not at all.

GUY: Oh.

TIM: No, tomorrow is our first day.

GUY: Oh. Looked to me like it should be your last day. [exit]

Half an hour later I went off to bed and all I could think about was this conversation.

Why did he think it was my last day? I stayed awake, thinking about this question. Then suddenly the answer hit me like a rocket: he misinterpreted our cause for celebration.

I was preparing the room so that my learners could have an engaging experience. He assumed that the enjoyment in learning begins when the learning finishes. But his logic is upside-down to me. It presupposes that learning is a chore. When the chore is complete, only then may we enjoy ourselves. This logic dominates the way that many people think about learning. I have attended five day conferences and on the final night everyone will go out and celebrate. When I ask why they are celebrating they say because it is the last night. What this means is that they are celebrating because it's all over. I reject the associations of learning with displeasure and the association of celebration with completion. I want to bring celebration into the whole learning experience.

People love to celebrate: birthdays; family events; parties. There is traditionally very little celebration within the learning event, but introducing even modest gestures of celebration can transform the atmosphere: maybe a round of applause; some positive feedback; shaking hands; or simply saying 'thank you' to one another in the room!

Clapping is a great way to raise the mood. Babies love to clap – when we clap, they clap back. It makes everyone feel happy, and it's a natural part of their development too. But when we get older this gesture loses its magic. A trainer once said to me: 'I'm running a session... but I really don't like doing all this clapping stuff, it feels a bit too American.' Try telling that to all UK pop stars and entertainers. Perhaps a rejection of clapping reveals a common expectation that reward should be used to inspire good results, in favour of using celebration to inspire good efforts. Reward is commonly used as an incentive for some learners. I was told at school that if I worked hard I would be rewarded with good test results. But because I did not even want to do any tests, (I had a phobia towards them) it made no sense for me to work hard.

On the one hand, rewards can really alienate some learners, and on the other hand they can induce a spirit of unhealthy competition. I have often seen competition introduced into learning sessions, and very often competition has the exact opposite effect of celebration. Fantastic sessions can be ruined as two groups compete against each other. Celebration can often foster collaboration but competition tends to foster distrust and anxiety. You only have to see the look on the faces of the winning and losing teams at a large football match to realise that only 50% will go away feeling successful.

Competitive approaches can work productively if it is clear to all learners that later on in the process everyone wins in the end. I once ran the final review component of a three day workshop. The group was divided into two teams, and each team was asked to generate five challenging questions around the material from the last three days of learning. At this point of the exercise even using the label 'team' signified there could be a winning and losing side. We sat the teams opposite each other in a confrontational configuration and asked them to reveal their questions. When each team had posed one question we intervened and radically shifted the focus of the exercise: instead of throwing the question to the other team, each team was responsible for coaching the opposing team to get the correct answers! They had generated some awful, devious questions because their assumption was that the winning team would be that which got the most questions right. But with the change of focus the competitive spirit was diffused and the atmosphere became much more collaborative.

When the process finished both groups had equal scores. We celebrated with handshakes and rousing music around the room.

This incident perfectly illustrates the contrast between two opposite learning paradigms: on the one hand a competitive environment which is driven by reward; on the other hand, a collaborative environment which is driven by celebration.
I know which kind of environment sounds more appealing to me! COME ON!

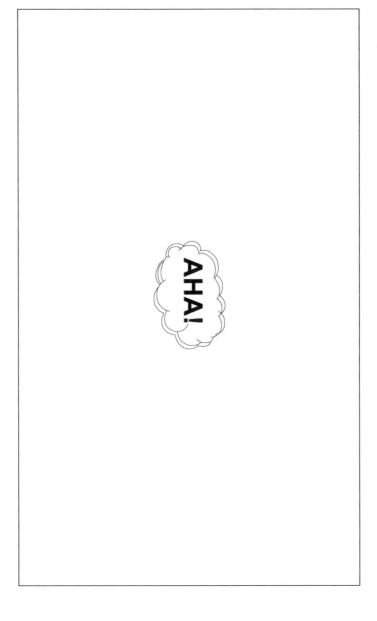

Do different

I recently had a client call me up and he said, 'Tim, we really want you to come in and work with a group of our people. We're really excited about this.' I said, 'That's great, but hang on a minute: you're running this event, you're getting people to attend from all over Europe so it's costing your business a lot of money – let's think carefully about the purpose. I'll send you a questionnaire to fill in.' So I e-mailed off the questionnaire, and it included this question: 'What do you want the group to be saying, thinking, doing different as a result of the programme?' He called me up and said, 'I find this question very difficult to answer.' I replied, 'Well, that's the one you really need to answer because if we don't have an understanding of what the 'do different' is after the session, then why are we running it?!'

Education can feel meaningless and boring unless it helps us to do something, or think differently in the future. So here are some questions for YOU: what are you going to 'do different' as a result of this book?

Has it just been a good read?
Will you recommend it to somebody else?
Are you going to try some of the processes?
Are you going to implement some of the techniques into your next presentation, teaching session or training event?

To help answer these questions, let's breeze through the information in this book to remind ourselves how we can do different in the future.

STRIKE A POSE – How are we going to build more purpose for our learners? How can we get them to take ownership of the information that we are delivering? How can we make the learning environment more safe by using safe language and safe practice? How can we get our group more engaged in the learning process?

To get more engaged in the process we might want to think about the SEVEN LEARNING TALENTS. There's the linguist talent, the mathematical/logical talent, the visual/spatial talent, the music/rhythm talent, the bodily/physical talent, the inter-personal talent, and the intra-personal talent. There are many ways that we can do things differently by appealing to these talents within our groups. Think about what YOUR talents are and what helps YOU to learn more effectively. This recognition can be a great starting point for implementing new approaches in the future.

Let's remember to get learners SETTLED. Think of the lunch party story in which people are filled full of food even though they are not ready to eat. Find out about your learners: why have they come along; what do they need to learn and what do they want to be thinking or saying when they leave?

It might help to do things differently if we remember to spell ENVIRONMENT WITH THREE 'P's. It's helpful to think about place but we need to think beyond the physical attributes of the training room – how we can apply the P.O.S.E. model and how we can ensure that our session will be successful by planning ahead.

How can we really maximise the short space of time that we share working with our group? How can we extend learning before the session with pre-exposure material? How can we get people to think about information before they even enter the room? And most importantly, how can we extend the learning AFTER the session? AND SOME MORE!

You may want to increase your performance and in turn the performance of your group, so start using LET'S LANGUAGE. Let's think about how we can engage groups by expressing ourselves through collaborative language, rather than try to sell them on 'I want you to do something for me.' Experiment with it, see if it works for your group!

I HAVE A SUGGESTION for the next 'do differently' – let's think about using more suggestive language. If we're using learning logs, let's make sure that our instructions are clear and that we keep suggesting how our learners can apply their learning outside of the training room. So let's start to use this suggestive language to make learning more lean and help people have more attention and recall in the future.

Let's start to plan our sessions around the WHAT and the HOW. Think about WHAT the group will be learning but also HOW they will absorb this new information. You may want to plan out the timings for the session and work out how much time you're spending on the WHAT and how much on the HOW. Most people tend to learn through the process and then link process to content, so think about how to make the HOW as vivid and as varied as possible.

Start to FRAME your session – create your introduction by using the F.R.A.M.E. model: focus on What's In It For Me?; how can it be relevant; how can your learners apply the information; how will they make meaning of the content; and close with an emotional recap. Practice by writing your frames for the session, sharing them with people or recording them. Framing the piece is as important as the piece itself, so spend as much time working on the frame as the content that is being delivered.

Next time you go to a meeting or presentation, watch how people react to the language and attitude modelled by the facilitator. Experiment by MODELLING good positive language and see what comes back from the group. Model key words and phrases and see if they start returning in your feedback session. Experiment with this – it can really work for you!

Use music, powerful language or get people to move about in order to create STATE CHANGES. Compile a list of the state changes that you can implement into your sessions. Build a record or a mindmap of changes that you have used in the past, and steal state changes from other people's sessions. See how it works and keep a record of what happens!

LESS IS MORE! Let's think about how we can keep the content down within the session. Remember the story of the seven chairs – train your spotlight on your learners and do not become preoccupied with your own need to unload information. Keep things as simple as possible - use the three 'S' model – Simplify, Simplify and Simplify once more. When you are asked questions, the three 'S' model will help you to avoid repeating explanations and help you to offer fresh descriptions.

Integrate CELEBRATION into your session. If people start to get competitive make sure that you have strategies to ensure that everybody is in a winning situation. Remember the football match where 50% of the fans go home happy and 50% go home unhappy. So celebrate learning by asking learners to write down what they have done well, how they are going to apply their learning, and ask them to share these insights with other people. Shake hands with learners, say 'thank you' for learning with us, and give people feedback when they have done well. People will start to model this – it's amazing!

So here are a few ideas that have changed the way that we look at learning and have had an impact throughout the world on many people. It's amazing how complex learning can be and it's amazing how learners can make it more complex for themselves. If we start to think about putting the spotlight on the learner it helps to make that process feel less complex and helps to make the learner feel they are taking away something useful and relevant. The spotlight needs to be on us when we do our planning and on how we're going to get our content across. But please, when you're out there – *turn the spotlight around on the groups.* Because it is absolutely invaluable to help people to learn something new and to help people to hold onto this learning for years.

My notes

-

-

-

-

-

Extending your learning

Books

Allen, Richard, *Impact Teaching*, Allyn & Bacon 2002
de Porter, Bobbi, *Quantum Learning*, Dell Publishing 1992
Gardner, Howard, *Multiple Intelligences*, Basic Books 1993
Harkin, Joe, Turner, Gill & Dawn, Trevor, *Teaching Young Adults*, Routledge Falmer 2001
Jackson, Paul & McKergow, Mark, *The Solutions Focus*, Nicholas Brearley Books 2002
Jensen, Eric, *Brain Based Learning*, The Brain Store Inc 1997
Meier, Dave, *The Accelerated Learning Book*, McGraw-Hill 2000

Websites

· www.stretchlearning.com
· www.eclo.org
· www.ialearn.org
· www.seal.org
· www.thesolutionsfocus.com

'As a result of the Stretch Learning workshop we have redesigned our European induction programme and incorporated a number of the ideas into other training material. The workshop was a breath of fresh air – stimulating, instructive and very practical.'

Rick Woodward, Learning and Development Director, Kimberly-Clark

'You are true consultants. You come in, deliver, enable, coach. We model your approach, have success, and then we eventually find that we don't need you any more – only your principles and techniques.'

Personnel Manager, a Global Manufacturing Company, Lisbon, Portugal

'I have often seen experienced and 'hardened' trainers (including myself!) successfully change their approach under Tim's inspirational and skilful guidance.'

Walter Blackburn, Managing Director, PeopleTrack

'Tim Andrews is one of the elite few that are able to understand, synthesize and apply learning principles in a smart, practical way.'

Eric Jensen, author of *Brain Based Learning*

'Tim's approach to the field of accelerated learning is exciting, dynamic and unique.'

Dr Rich Allen, author of *Impact Teaching*, Big Fork, Montana

'Tim Andrews is a learning champion – his talents help others to see different views of the world and of themselves.'

Glen Capelli, True Learning Centre, Western Australia

'We have adopted the ideas and principles of Stretch Learning within the global roll-out of our Change programme for Diageo. The results have been nothing short of monumental.'

Peter Brook, Director of DWBB with Customers Diageo

Index